Gold Star Referral Clubs

Gold Star Referral Clubs help business people and professionals grow their businesses **without** large advertising outlays.

Local businesses can access a business growth system that delivers the power of word-of-mouth advertising to their bottom lines.

Headquartered in Tulsa, Oklahoma, Gold Star Referral Clubs was started by Beth and Todd Davis in 2007 and is considered the finest business networking organization in the country, growing to over 100 locations nationwide. We lost Beth to cancer in 2019.

Chief Executive Officer, Todd Davis is a savvy business leader with expertise in business networking, relationship strategies, and club growth. He is greatly responsible for Gold Star's expansion. On any given day, you can find Todd on the phone counseling members or helping the next, very excited Gold Star Director launch his first club.

"The benefit of membership in Gold Star is that you can grow your business with new customers through qualified, ready-to-do-business referrals. However, members also benefit from associating with other motivated and like-minded business people. These relationships translate into long-term reciprocal relationships. That's why our clubs work so well!"

We have an extensive training system that helps members and new Directors put their businesses on the fast track to referrals.

Gold Star Referral Clubs started at the request of a friend, a Financial Advisor. He was locked out of another business networking organization. It didn't take long to start, and word soon spread about the "Gold Star Difference." Within a year, Gold Star Clubs were getting established across the country.

We invite you to grow your business with Gold Star Clubs.

BUSINESS NETWORKING

Over 90% of people surveyed prefer to be referred to a professional when they need a product or service and over 75% of those said that they used the person they were referred to.

We help you create a never-ending stream of referrals.

Develop relationships with fellow business people who will gladly and consistently do business with you and refer clients, friends, and relatives to *YOU*. Business networking with Gold Star WORKS!

It's a fun, yet serious way to grow your business.

Stories From Business
Professionals Who Give
Before They Receive

Gold Star

Referral Clubs

For

Beth Davis

and

Darlene Shortridge

Contents

Foreword... 1

Todd Davis 5

Margy Pezdirtz 17

Patti Edwards 25

Sybil Hale 35

Sandy Jones.................................. 45

Brett Lorton................................. 55

David Nixon................................. 63

Dawna Terrell............................... 73

Danielle Hill................................ 83

Nathan Acker 91

Caleb Jackson 99

Courtney Wilson.......................... 107

Michael McGinley......................... 113

Darlene Shortridge 121

The Gold Star Difference............... 131

Foreword

Todd Davis, Founder - Gold Star Clubs

This book aims to give the reader an idea about what Gold Star Clubs are, how it works, how they can benefit, and stories from professionals who have shared their success.

Our story began in 2003 when my now late wife, Beth, and I were in another networking group. We represented our real estate business. After years of service there, I got tired of having a thumb on my neck every time I turned around. Rules for this, rules for that, don't do this, and forget about doing that.

Don't be confused. Gold Star Clubs has rules. Only we're a little nicer about them. Our heart is for our members to succeed.

We left that networking group late in 2006 to focus on our new Real Estate Company, Alliance Team Realty.

In early 2007, one of my agents introduced us to a guy who wanted to sell his online directory listings. He mentioned that since the guys in the previous group were no longer a choice, he suggested, "You know about that networking stuff, why not start your own group?"

One of Beth's traits was being a research nut. She looked high and low to find something from another company that matched our hearts, and she could not.

After discussing the idea, we decided to move forward. We knew referrals were better than leads, and referrals had worked for us before.

In real estate, there are a lot of people that, in essence, are needed to have a successful transaction. We reached out to anyone and everyone we already did business with and asked them to consider joining our new endeavor. Almost all our tradespeople came along.

On August 1st, 2007, we officially launched our first Club.

By August 15th, several other tradespeople came to us; they said, "You are industry exclusive, and my spot has been taken already. Can you start my friends and me in another group?"

By the launch of the third Club, we realized we had built a method, just as in real estate, where everything was part of a system. That Club system could get applied to professionals in the workforce who wanted to do more business by referrals.

Part of our system relied on the members to help grow the Club. If they invited business people they already knew and did business with, the Club would grow to sustainable levels quickly.

The best part of Gold Star Clubs is that we have shorter meetings, pass real ready-to-do-business referrals, have much more fun than other similar groups, and have a no-contract monthly fee.

We also don't require bringing a referral to every meeting. We want our referrals to be where the person who needs help with a product or service is expecting the call from the person who can provide the help.

If you don't have a Gold Star Club near you, consider reaching out to me. Let's see if you are qualified to start your own Club. It's a compensated position, meaning we pay you to promote your business. Most importantly, we're successful because our system works!

Best of success,

Todd Davis

Chief Executive Officer
Gold Star Referral Clubs
www.goldstarclubs.com
More Business for Your Business, by Referrals

Todd Davis

Founder/CEO

Gold Star Referral Clubs

goldstarclubs.com

7170 S Braden Ave., Suite 165
Tulsa, OK 74136

(918) 933-4866

todd@goldstarclubs.com

Like so many of the stories we hear from our Gold Star members, I didn't start out to be the founder of a referral club. My late wife, Beth, and I just slid into it – not necessarily by accident but by following through on a suggestion from an acquaintance. I was a Realtor and enjoyed the life it provided for us, but I also knew the importance of meeting people and getting referrals.

My dad was a Lt. Colonel in the Army Reserves. He was a chemist by trade and worked at a civilian job later in life as a contractor to the Air Force, analyzing nuclear bombs. My mom had been in the WACs for a brief time but when we kids – three of us – two boys, and a sister – arrived, she became a stay-at-home wife and mother. My parents moved to Washington and that is where I grew up, finished high school, and started a career. A few years later, I met my wife – Beth– and we started a life together. My background was in the restaurant business and then in real estate in the Washington area.

We were and are Christians, and that is how we ended up in Tulsa. One morning Beth came out of the shower and said, "Do you think we should check out Rhema Bible School in Tulsa?" I wasn't even sure where Tulsa was, but we booked a flight and made our way to Oklahoma. We have been here ever since. We got our certificates from Rhema and served for several years as Chaplains to the Sheriff's Department, ministering to the deputies, not to the prisoners.

It wasn't long before I was back in the real estate world which I loved and was very successful at. As an agent, I worked out my own system for meeting with buyers and sellers. My pattern was to meet with them in my office or at their home for at least an hour and a half before I ever showed them a house.

I wanted to get to know them to understand what it was they really wanted in a home. Once the relationship was developed it was easy to get them to sign up with me as their broker and I took it from there, finding the perfect home for them and closing on it in a rapid manner. During the crazy time in 2007 and 2008, our success model was 'sign-up to sold in 44 days' when the average agent ran almost four to five months. Everyone was happy and satisfied. For sellers, the very same tactic. I got to know the clients and help them move on to what they wanted.

> The unexpected has a habit of showing up in our lives. How we handle it will decide the future for ourselves, our families, and our businesses.

To help my real estate career, I joined a networking/referral club and attended for several years. I enjoyed meeting people and networking with them, but the club was replete with rules concerning everything. It was beginning to feel like there was a stranglehold on me. There was no kindness or consideration for the members and after a prolonged time, I found it not only annoying but rude. I was beginning to lose interest in the club because of the rules, regs and rudeness and finally pulled out of it.

By now, our real estate business had boomed. We were experiencing enormous success but there was still that desire to belong to a referral group that actually worked but proved itself to be user-friendly as well. A friend suggested I start one of my own since I had had so many years of experience as a member of the other club. He reminded me that I knew what worked, what didn't work, and what made members feel happy to be a part of an organization. I didn't really want to do it, but Beth was open to it. She was an ardent researcher, and she did her due diligence in searching for a referral club that would meet the standards we felt were necessary. There were none.

We decided to do it but to do it with heart and compassion. We would establish rules – for sure – but they would be rules that were honest, and people could live with. We would need to limit membership to being industry-specific, meaning that only one person from each industry could join a specific club. This way you didn't have twenty-five realtors and one banker showing up and expecting to grow their business. It just didn't work that way. We also knew we wanted to keep the clubs relatively small with industry-specific members.

Within no time, we had all our slots filled, and people were coming to us saying, "You filled my slot and I want to belong. Why don't you start another club." We did. We quickly grew from one to three and then more. We knew there had to be a fee to belong to the club because people tend to get out of something what they put into it. No fee equaled no referrals and no business growth. That wasn't our goal. We set up a membership fee that was reasonable and easily recouped if people were getting and giving genuine referrals.

I came to realize that our members needed a little teaching on how to do a legitimate referral. It didn't work just to tell someone to go see Mary Jane at the local shoe store because her roof leaked, or her plumbing was backed up. That would be a dead end for sure. A successful referral would be when the member told Mary Jane about a person they knew that was a great roofer/plumber or whatever she needed and asked her permission for the person to contact her. Then, I would tell the service person about Mary Jane, supply her information on a professional-looking printed slip of paper, and tell them Mary Jane was expecting them to call. A strong referral bridge was built and would, most likely, become a great success for all.

Another thing I have always been strong on is the 1-2-1 meeting. To have a great 1-2-1 meeting, it should be one-way. The person requesting the meeting should do so because he/she really wants to know about the other person and is willing to attentively listen to them. If it is a two-way meeting, the inviter will be sitting there listening and waiting for their turn to talk about themselves. Therefore, they'll be less engaged in listening and more into arranging their presentation of themselves and their business. To be successful at a 1-2-1 meeting, I strongly recommend it be in a quiet location – maybe your office if you have one, or their office. If neither of you have an office, then a coffee shop or the like is good but be sure to choose one that is quiet.

Be prepared to listen. You want to learn about this person you've invited to the 1-2-1. It is about them, not you. You'll have your moment. If you build a strong bridge with your invitee, there will be more meetings in the future and probably a long-lasting friendship, which is what we really want.

I have seen several of our club members obtain a degree of success through Gold Star they had only dreamed of. One of those people is Jerry Banker, my

AC man. Jerry was brought to Gold Star by a plumber friend of his, a guy named Ivan.

Jerry was reluctant, saying, "These things don't work. I'm not ever going to be a part of it," insisting that he wasn't going to do it. Ivan prevailed, telling Jerry to shut up and pay the dues. Jerry did that, probably reluctantly.

In the first quarter of the year he joined, Jerry made $800, so it more than paid for his first-year membership. His second full year, he made over 60 grand, directly from Gold Star members and referrals. His third year, he went over $100,000 and he has never looked back. Now Jerry has a second representative of his AC business who is attending another club, continuing to grow the business through referrals.

But this isn't the only success story. There are many. Some of them are so large it's mind-boggling. An example of how a good Gold Star Referral Club can help grow a business, if done correctly, is the example of two guys who are in two different clubs. One of them is a computer repair guru who built all our computers for us. He is great. He can handle up to fifteen or more computers, working on the same network. The other guy is an IT guy. He can manage hundreds of computers all at once without any difficulty. Both are members of Gold Star. They work well together, and refer each other to clients, never pointing out they are from two different businesses.

They write and bill the client and take care of the finances themselves without ever causing any conflict or consternation for their clients. It works seamlessly and is good for everyone.

One of our largest clubs is in Modesto, California. A college professor type guy started it and the club was beginning to grow but he was offered a teaching position and his wife insisted he take it. I wanted to find someone who could take the club over and keep it going. Ta-Da! Mary Matthews, one of the members, stepped up and said she wanted to do it.

In that situation, Mary was perfect. She does sales for iHeart Radio, and she understands marketing. She meets a lot of people and invites them to join Gold Star because ads are one way of getting your name out there. It is a great connection for her and for us. Mary is now a Regional Director and continues to grow Gold Star in her region with the idea of retiring from her job and going full-time with us. We don't push her; we applaud her and make sure she knows we are here to help if she needs us.

We are in seven states now. Our goal is to have at least one Gold Star Referral Club in the larger centers of each state. It is an obtainable goal. To grow a Gold Star Club and have it work for you as well as your members, you must be intentional, reach out and invite people to attend. It isn't enough that you just show up at meetings, although that is required, but you take part.

Learn how to stand up and do a sixty-second presentation about you, your business, and what you are looking for. Take the training to learn how to efficiently and effectively do a ten-minute presentation that teaches others about what you do, how your organization works, and why they – as well as you – should be excited about what you do.

I am out of the real estate business now and full force into Gold Star. I know what this organization has done for me, and I want to see it do the same for others. Someday I may retire, but not for a while.

Beth passed away in June 2019 after twenty-five years of marriage. I didn't think I would ever remarry, in fact that wasn't even on my radar. But God intervened. Through a mutual acquaintance named Cindy, I met my wife, Joni. We have been married just over a year and we are incredibly happy together. Joni and her dog, Rachel, a poodle, moved here from California and made their home with me. We are building our future together and enjoying it. We have adopted two more dogs, Australian Shepherds, whom we named Cali and Paris. You can figure out why those names.

I love to fish and have my own boat which is easily spotted by the number of fishing poles standing in the stern of the boat. One just never knows what lure he might need out there in the fresh waters of Oklahoma! I also enjoy sport shooting, whether it is with a pistol or a long gun. Joni is now learning to shoot, and I look forward to our doing it together soon.

The unexpected has a habit of showing up in our lives and how we handle it will decide the future for ourselves, our families, and our businesses. I find being intentional in what we do is important, whether it is in the way we work, the way we socialize, or the way we grow our business. Gold Star Referral Club is intentional for those who want to grow and develop their business. We hope you'll come along and join a club near you.

Like real estate, Gold Star has a proven system that works, if you work it.

Margy Pezdirtz

Brand Ambassador

40 Day Publishing

40DayPublishing.com

PO Box 950794
Oklahoma City, OK 73195

405-833-6092

margy.pezdirtz@40daypublishing.com

As far back as I can remember, I have been an ardent reader of any kind of book I could get my hands on. I attended grade school in rural Oklahoma where I was honored to be the president of our school's early reader program which allowed us to buy our own paperbacks for pennies. I loved and devoured the Detective Nancy Drew books, reading each of them more than once. Fast forward more years than I can count, and I am still buying my own paper backs, but this time I am the author.

I am not sure when I first picked up a pencil and paper and started writing. I was probably writing a letter of protest to our school principal or someone on my Big Chief tablet. It doesn't really matter. I was always writing something for someone, or myself, or maybe for my dolls. Our lives often wind a circuitous path until we finally find the straight path that we were created to walk, and it has been no different for me.

My family comes from solid, Oklahoma stock. My grandfather rode in the opening of the Cherokee Strip in 1893 and was the first to break the sod on his homestead in Grant County, in northern Oklahoma. That is where we grew up, on my parents' farm surrounded by family, animals, and long days in the summer sun. To this day I have a love for that part of Oklahoma where the soil is rich and BLACK, not red. There is something absolutely, gloriously beautiful about a farmer putting a small seed into the ground and trusting that seed to grow into a crop that will feed his family. That is faith. Watching the golden stream of wheat flow from the auger of a combine into a truck bin is a beautiful testimony of that faith.

In the years after leaving the farm, my life has been busy with getting married, having children, and attending college. Over a winter break during my college years, I picked up a book by James Michener called The Source, and my life began to change. The book told the story of an archeology dig in Israel and as the layers of soil were gently brushed away, the story of Israel took root in my soul. That was in January 1967. Six months later, the Six Day War broke out and my knowledge of Israel, at that time, was limited to what I had read in that book. But I knew I wanted Israel to win that war. She won! Little did I know then that I would one day live there, meet my soul mate—also a Christian—and travel back to the Land so many times. My life has been blessed because I chose to read a book by a man whom I would never know but whose writing impacted my life.

In 1971, I had an up close and real encounter with my God when I accepted Jesus as my personal savior and have been on that path ever since. Because of Him, I have been given the opportunity to live on both coasts as well as a great deal of international travel. My journey in life has been influenced by my Lord, the word of God, and the people of Israel, which has been the passion of my story telling in teaching the word and writing about it, particularly the heroines of the Bible whom we hear little about.

For several years after my husband passed away, I traveled for Christian Friends of Israeli Communities (CFOIC) talking in churches and teaching about Israel today and how important she is to us as a country and as believers. I met wonderful people with like hearts and minds who understood their Bible as I did. As I taught, I was encouraged by my audience to put my teachings into writing. I knew I had to do that, but I didn't know in what form.

> "And I will bless those who bless you, And the one who curses you I will curse. And in you all the families of the earth will be blessed." Genesis 12:3

After authoring a book of my own, I was introduced to the publishing world with all its foibles, challenges, frustrations, and finally - rewards. My first book sustained a powerful array of seventeen rejects from publishers—most of whom sent it back unopened and unread even though I had jumped through every hoop they requested. Despair hit hard with the 'Now what' questions running through my mind. If I was supposed to do this, as I felt I was, why was it being rejected? It wasn't until years later that I had the wonderful privilege of meeting and getting to know Dan and Darlene (Shortridge) Mawhinney of 40 Day Publishing.

Darlene spoke at an Oklahoma Writer's Federation event that I was attending, and she made more sense to me than any person I had ever met in the writing arena. I bought their book, 40 Day Publishing, then hired them to publish my book. It was so great to have a publisher that cared—that would help and give advice. For the first time in years, I was finally on the path that had been set before me and it was a straight one. Over the years, Dan and Darlene became close friends with dinners, parties, and long conversations. I began doing a little ghost writing for them as a favor to both of us.

When Darlene suddenly and unexpectedly passed away in September 2022, Dan asked if I would come alongside him as the Brand Ambassador for 40 Day Publishing and help him continue to grow the business they had started together. It was and is an honor to be a viable part of 40 Day Publishing.

I love meeting people, talking to them about their life and their book ideas. It is wonderful to see the hope and wonder in their eyes as they speak about the possibility of finally writing the book. Until now, it has only been a dream or a silent hope, but they are beginning to visualize it happening. It is a pleasure to see that possibility grow into reality. It is an amazing experience to see the joy on their face when they see their book in print for the first time.

Everyone has a story. Most people do not think they do, but they do. Every life counts and that story needs to be written for posterity if for only their family. I often tell the story of finding eight handwritten pages my dad had written about his life, his growing up on the farm, his school years, how he met my mom, and the names and birthdates of his brothers and sisters. He was not a famous author, nor did he desire to be, but he felt compelled to sit down one night and write his story. I love it and I am so thankful to have it. Now I am doing the same thing for my children, and I am incorporating my dad's story into mine. As I said, everyone has a story. They should write that story as a catharsis and as a blessing to their families that will be there long after they are gone.

We are here to help you tell your story. You don't have to be a practiced author to write it or tell it. If you want to tell your story in a way that others can read -- besides your family -- we are here to help you do that as well. We make publishing easy, and we do believe, really believe, that everyone has a story to tell. We are here to help you tell your story well.

Patti Edwards

Owner/President

Heartland Claims Consulting

heartlandclaimsconsulting.com

PO Box 20831
Oklahoma City, OK 73156

405-513-3146

patti@heartlandclaimsconsulting.com

I am a detective. I do not work for the police department, nor do I wear a badge or carry a gun, but I am a detective all the same. "What" you might ask, "am I talking about?" My primary job is to help chiropractors with their insurance billing by finding out why they are getting rejections on claims filed. No kidding. This is as intense and specific as trying to solve a crime but there is no crime, no blood, no dead bodies, just insurance papers lying around looking for understanding. Enter me. But it was not always like this…

I am one of those rare people who grew up in the major metropolis of Sturgis, South Dakota, which boasts a normal population of just over 7,000 residents most of the year – that is until the nine-day Sturgis Motorcycle Rally ascends upon our small town. Then our sleepy community explodes to well over 500,000 people with bikers coming from all parts of the country to take part in the rally. I was an eighteen-year-old kid selling tee shirts at the Harley Davidson Museum when the 50th Annual Black Hills Motorcycle Rally roared into town. It was an interesting, fun, and challenging experience meeting so many people from innumerable backgrounds. They told stories and I listened. Their stories confirmed my desire to experience other parts of our country.

Sturgis was not a bad place to grow up. We had a normal family life, attending church and enjoying family and friends. My parents divorced when I was two years old with each remarrying and giving me four half-siblings. Our blended family life was not too different from so many others and, like young people everywhere, I was eager to get away, be on my own and try my wings. As soon as I graduated from high school I left South Dakota for Edmond, Oklahoma to attend school at Oklahoma Christian University (OCU). I have been in Oklahoma ever since.

I met my husband, Doug, at OCU my freshman year. He came from Granite City, Illinois, to attend the same university. Our first date was a week before Thanksgiving, 1990 and we were married the following June 1991. We set aside our college careers to start a business -- GAMMA Laser Supply -- remanufacturing laser toner cartridges. Doug took care of the remanufacturing part and I managed sales, bookkeeping, and customer relations. We were successful enough that by the time our first child, Hunter, was born in 1995, I was able to be a stay-at-home mom which continued through the birth of our second child, Blair, three years later.

By now, we were living in Piedmont, Oklahoma, where we were members of the Church of Christ. There wasn't a Church of Christ in Piedmont, so we found ourselves driving into Oklahoma City to attend services. We wanted more than that. We wanted a local church where our children could attend and grow up with other children of the same faith and we could have fellowship with church families. Together with like-minded couples we started a home fellowship with the idea of growing into an official church. Over the years the little fellowship did grow into a full-blown church and with it came all the challenges and complications of any growing congregation which also created stress for us as a couple.

After fourteen years of owning and running GAMMA Laser Supply, Doug wanted to change occupations and go into nursing. Our children were now old enough that I could comfortably go back to work and help him through nursing school which I did from 2007 through 2011, selling home and auto insurance for a firm in Piedmont. After Doug graduated from nursing school and was working in his new career, things got much easier for us financially so I was able to stop working. Our daughter wanted to homeschool, and we were happy to be able to accommodate her. Blair finished high school and married right afterward, setting up her own home. She was out on her own as was our son Hunter, leaving me with an empty nest which really did not need any further fluffing. It wasn't long before boredom began to set in, and I started looking for something to do.

Because I had worked in the insurance business and understood – to some degree – insurance billing, claims, EOBs, and the other finer parts of the insurance arena, I knew I had a niche, but I didn't really want to go back into selling. I heard of a chiropractor in our area that might have an opening as a billing clerk, working with insurance. I inquired and got the job working one day a week, on Fridays, when the office was closed. This gave me time to learn the software program and the process of billing for a chiropractor's office. Soon I found out I was good at it and enjoyed it so I began to reach out to other chiropractors.

> # A lot of a little is a lot.

To further my knowledge, I watched several chiropractors, learning their procedures and how it affected the bodies of their clients as well as how it related to insurance billing. I realized they were not billing for all the techniques they were practicing, which caused them to miss added payment from the insurance companies. I consulted with the doctors on the procedures they were not billing so they could update their billing practices to match with their work.

In no time, I had two other chiropractors I was working for as an employee one day a week. Then I met Chandra Ford, the wife and office manager of a chiropractor in Bethany, Oklahoma. I talked to her about doing their billing and she posed a question I had not considered, "How much do you charge per claim?"

Until now, I had been working as a W-2 employee, not a contractor. I found out from her that they were using a billing firm out of Florida but really wanted to use someone locally. I asked for the name of the Florida company, asking permission to get back with her on Friday with an answer to her question.

As with all good investigators, I did my homework and when I returned to speak with Ms. Ford. I was now a self-employed contractor with an eye on the future as an independent businesswoman and Heartland Claims Consulting was born. I hired an accountant, became incorporated, and changed the entire way I billed my clients. I was no longer a W-2 employee. I was a self-employed businessperson, and I was excited about the future. One that I was building for myself.

I came to understand I had an innate ability to dig into the billing of various chiropractors. Although they used different software programs, I was able to discover missing claims along with those that were denied by insurance companies as duplicate claims. They were not duplicate claims, they were just wrongly coded. That was when I began to feel like a detective digging through clues to solve problems that would help the doctors and, in doing so, help me build my own business.

By this time, I was a single-again woman responsible for my own living and future. I was excited over what that future held but knew I needed to continue to grow my business. I had attended Toastmasters and learned how to organize my presentation, to be professional about my talk, and confident in approaching potential clients. It was time to reach out and really grow.

Enter Gold Star Referral Clubs. My friend invited me to attend the club in Edmond and I was eager to go. But it was a breakfast club forty-five minutes away from home. I'm not normally an early morning person and getting to that club from my home was pushing me quite a bit because of traffic. Then, I learned of the Uptown Gold Star Referral Club, which is only about seven minutes from home. Here I am. I have been part of the Uptown club ever since and I love it.

Being a single-again woman has been an adjustment for me, one that has left me feeling a little stymied when it comes to business things, like buying a home on my own. A realtor friend was able to guide me through the purchase of a home. In the process, prior to completing the sale, I hired one of the Gold Star members to inspect the home for me to make sure I knew what I was getting into.

The other members are delightfully wonderful, welcoming and have quickly become friends. I have gained four more chiropractors through the referrals of Gold Star members and I have been pleased and honored to refer members to others for their areas of expertise. It is comforting to know I can refer these honest businesspeople to others without wondering if they will be fair in pricing and in the work done. With Gold Star, I have no qualms about referring the members of Uptown Gold Star for work. I am thankful for Gold Star, the training I have received through this organization, and the improvement of my outreach skills which have come about through the auspices of the Gold Star club.

Sybil Hale

Founder/Owner

Pros Make Ready

prosmakeready.com

5200 Colfax Place
Oklahoma City, OK 73112

405-777-3216

sybil@prosmakeready.com

I had a boss for nine years—nine long years of being told what to do, when to do it, how to do it, and for how long to do it. I don't know about you, but I'm a type A personality. Type A's like to be the ones telling other people what to do. You can imagine my dilemma.

After working for six different bosses, I'd had enough. I had two children, and my life was consumed by a J.O.B. and I wanted my life back.

I have a brother who is an entrepreneur and while I thought of him having his own business was a cool idea, I never considered doing the same. When the company I was working for filed bankruptcy, the owner suggested I start my own business, a cleaning service.

That was a firm no. NO. I was not interested in being someone else's boss or being responsible for them putting food on their table. I had enough problems figuring my own life out. I didn't need the hassle.

He knew me well and knew when he said, "Sybil, imagine working when you want so you can spend more time with your husband and sons?" He had my attention.

I saw what went into a business. There were physical buildings to maintain and employees to contend with. Separately, they can be overwhelming. Together? Downright scary. The drama in an office can be consuming. I had personal experience in that arena, and I didn't want any part of it. There are some things that are more important than convenience and doing what makes us comfortable.

I took my former boss' advice and started cleaning houses.

I live humbly. I'm not rich. I've never had the big house with the pool and the gardens. My little two-bedroom house would take me three hours—tops—to clean. Then again, let's be honest, we always get distracted when we're cleaning our own homes so maybe cut that time in half—from top to bottom it probably took me an hour and a half to two hours to clean.

I secured my first two houses immediately. Both were about three times the size of the one I was living in. You can imagine my overwhelm when I sat down with Mrs. Aspen and interviewed to clean her six thousand square foot home. She saw my heart in that interview and while I didn't have the experience to back my business up, she saw my desire to serve. She hired me on the spot.

For the first five years, I cleaned and served where I was planted. I enjoyed setting my own hours and I found myself recommending other service providers. I didn't realize I was networking, but that is exactly what I was doing.

I found I had so much business I couldn't do it all on my own, especially if I wanted to continue setting my own schedule and living life to the fullest. I started taking on contractors to help me clean. Mainly, other women and men who also had families and other responsibilities who wanted to earn some extra money.

It wasn't too much longer that I found the business that I built from scratch—and loved—turning into what I originally feared, something that consumed me and brought me very little joy. The powers that be decided, I had employees rather than contractors and wanted me to operate as a W-2 business rather than a 1099 contractor-based business. I fought it as long as I could.

In case you aren't aware, the government has an endless supply of money when it suits them. The key words are, when it suits them. They had far more resources than I did so my CPA recommended I restructure. I listened to my CPA. I completely changed how I did business and offered to teach anyone cleaning for me to run their own businesses. I then gave them most of my clients' accounts for multiple reasons: to lighten my load, to make sure my clients were well taken care of, and to give those dedicated, hardworking folks a way to keep money flowing in for their own families. I went back to just me doing what I loved and serving the people I had the honor to serve. Life was good.

If there is one guarantee in life, it's nothing stays the same. Or perhaps I should say, it shouldn't stay the same. If we aren't growing and experiencing change, the odds are, we are in a rut and have grown stagnant. I didn't want to be stagnant. Stagnant is a murky pond with green algae and weird critters roaming beneath the surface.

God planted an idea in my heart. I cleaned and I cleaned…but did I get rid of the weird critters—the ones I couldn't see—roaming beneath the surface? Were the homes I cleaned really clean?

It was August of 2019 when the idea began taking root. By October 15, I had transitioned from the surface cleaning of houses to killing the germs, viruses, allergens, odors, mold, and mildew that we can't always see but we know are lurking in every nook and cranny of our homes and workplaces. I knew to be productive we all need spaces that are superior, safe, and sanitary to work and live in.

I had no idea just four short months later, a worldwide epidemic would stop the world from spinning. God knew. When businesses shut down and people were fearful of an unknown virus—and rightly so—God knew I would still need the lights on, the mortgage paid, that food would still need to appear on the family table each night. He had a plan for me. Since that day, I have helped tens of thousands of individuals lead healthier lives.

In April 2019, 920,000 employees called in sick. One year later, that number skyrocketed to 2.02 million.

These numbers meant families had less income and more stress and worry added to their daily lives. Businesses had less workers on any given day and were stretched beyond their natural ability to serve. Between allergies, colds, viruses, etc.—basically, germs—more people were calling in sick than ever before. In fact, employers lost 225.8 billion dollars annually from injured and sick employees. Every day my company helps reduce those numbers.

> ## All THINGS are POSSIBLE through CHRIST who STRENGTHENS me!

Angie owns a daycare center. In January of 2020, she told me she wanted to try our services and she was giving me a year to prove our service would reduce the number of colds, viruses and so much more. Have you been around children? Have you seen some of the things they do? Yes, they share their sippy cups. But first, they pick their noses, then they pick each other's noses, and then they…okay, you get the idea. If only it ended there. They share everything, and I mean everything with one another. They put everything in their mouths. I've seen my grandson pick up a piece of chewed gum and attempt to eat it. How kids live past the age of six months I'll never know.

It was flu season, so we started by going every week. When kids stay home, parents stay home. When parents stay home, they don't make the money they need to live, and the daycare loses money. You can see how this could be a win-win for everyone involved.

During the first visit, we treated both the HVAC system (the air we breathe which needs to be treated a minimum of every six months) and sanitized the premises (which we did weekly). The results were beyond anything this daycare owner could have hoped for. Here is what she had to say,

"January of 2020, my childcare facility was going through the flu/RSV viruses that run rampant at that time of year. Sybil told me about her new sanitation service. It was time to try something to help the children and the parents. She started fogging the facility weekly. Then Covid hit. Through 2020 and beyond, we had two cases of strep throat and only one employee Covid case and it did not spread to any children or any other employees. "With the fogging being a regular part of our cleaning routine, we never closed our doors or had any outbreaks. I thank God for Sybil being proactive in helping us stay safe and sanitized."

In February of 2022, I checked in with her to see how her February attendance rates had changed from the previous years. She told me, "Prior to using your service, we averaged a 50 percent absence rate for the month of February. Since using your service, we are now at a 12% absence rate."

Those numbers are incredible and completely speak for themselves. I absolutely love that I have been given the opportunity to be a superhero every single time I am able to go into people's homes and businesses to protect them from the very things that can keep them down. The looks on their faces—the pure relief and gratefulness—is a reward that never grows old.

I joined Gold Star Referral Groups more than six years ago and being part of this organization has been the catalyst for me being such a connector of people. I am truly thankful for every opportunity that has come my way because of the relationships I have formed within my own club, cross clubbing in other area clubs, and Gold Star as a whole. I give the organization, Gold Star, the credit as to why I am now THE NETWORKING QUEEN! I cannot imagine I'd be where I am today without being a member.

Visit our website and watch the two-minute video to see us in action. Afterward, let's have a conversation so you can learn about leading a healthier, more productive life. Cleaner fresher air equals less sick time and more fun time for you.

Sandy Jones

Independent Beauty Consultant

Mary Kay Consultant

marykay.com/sjones92578

1804 Eagle Drive
Edmond, OK 73034

405-388-9044

sandymy3sons@gmail.com

This is the second time I have done this business.

Yes. You heard me correctly. I was in my early twenties, married with an eighteen-month-old son, Jay, from a previous marriage, when my husband, Dennis, was transferred to Bakersfield, CA. The distance factor from Kansas to Bakersfield, CA was an issue for all involved causing me to have to return to Kansas every three months for three weeks so his birth father could have visitation rights. Let me tell you, that was a challenge for all of us.

My husband and I had been high school sweethearts. We dated through our teen years, broke up and went our separate ways, only to get back together years later. We both had lived life enough to know when you find someone that is your soulmate, you need to grab on to them. We did that, comfortable in the knowledge that we understood each other's roots and we would make our life together work.

I had been using Mary Kay cosmetics for a while when my mother-in-law offered me the Mary Kay opportunity. I wasn't interested in selling anything, so my answer was an immediate and adamant, "NO!" But, living in California, away from family and friends, I felt the need to meet other women and develop relationships, plus adding money to our income to help cover the cost of my frequent trips to Kansas. My husband was in management in the oil and gas industry and had to travel, leaving me at home with our toddler.

Dennis' work required us to be frequently transferred from one state to another – I guess it is a good way to see America on the company's dime. But that didn't solve my loneliness issue. Mary Kay could.

My mother-in-law was happy to provide more information and reassured me that I could do the business if I applied myself. One of the advantages that I saw in Mary Kay was that it was as mobile as I was, allowing me to take it anywhere that we were transferred to. I needed flexibility so I signed up. The next time I went to Kansas for the required three-week stay, I took my showcase and products with me to work in my old stomping grounds in Hill City, in the NW corner of Kansas where not much happened. Working with Mary Kay there would break the monotony and give me the opportunity to reconnect with people I grew up with in this farming community.

Five years later we were transferred to our new location in Monahans, TX, arriving there in the middle of the night. The next morning, we eagerly opened the door of the hotel room to check out our new environment, and all we saw was desert – miles and miles of desert. There was scrub brush, mesquite, and dirt that blew in the slightest wind along with endless nothingness. The population was 6,953 at the 2010 census so you can imagine what it was 40 years ago! Dennis and I had serious discussions about where we had landed and why.

By now, our second child, Riley, was one year old. I didn't know if there would be a daycare available let alone a Mother's Day Out program. Our realtor, who became our friend, stepped up to the plate and helped me with solutions to those needs. Because my husband often had to be gone, I was left with a great deal of time on my hands, even with two children. There had been challenges with getting Jay into school in Monahans, but we mastered them. He had attended a private school in California because the schools there were a mess, even in those ancient days.

> ## If you help enough people receive what they want, you will receive what *you* want.

I found out that different school districts used different terms that none of us were familiar with, including my son. The Monahans school officials didn't think Jay should be in the advanced program because we were from California, and they judged us accordingly. I guess they thought we were some weirdos or something. In the long run, things worked out and Jay was in the advanced class the next semester. Maybe we weren't so weird after all.

When we left California, I had a team of ladies working with me in Mary Kay so I divided my customers up amongst them thinking they would continue building their businesses. It didn't happen that way. Eventually they all quit, leaving me without anyone to take care of my former customers. This was prior to the current tech generation with cell phones just beginning to come on the scene, usually affixed to your car. There wasn't any logical or feasible way I could take care of them from Texas, so I had to let that leg of my business go.

I set to work in Monahans and in no time, my business was thriving again. I knew how to work the Mary Kay way and I continued doing so, even though we were expecting another baby—our third. Wouldn't you know it, we got transferred again – this time to Ft. Smith, Arkansas. I was in my last trimester and the doctor wasn't letting me leave Texas. Dennis was able to delay his departure for a short time but had to leave Texas two weeks after Taylor was born. Not only did I now have three children, one of whom was a newborn, but I was left with showing and selling the house. The market was flat, with few sales leaving us in a quandary as to what to do. Eventually, the house sold at a loss for us. Once again, I divided my clients up amongst the girls I had on my team and headed northeast to Ft. Smith, believing this time they would take care of the customers I had given them. Not!

Ft. Smith was much prettier as far as the state was concerned, but we were facing the same issues. I had to find a pediatrician for the boys, get Jay into a private school and find a Mother's Day Out program in our new city. We lived in Arkansas for a year and a half before we were transferred again, this time to Oklahoma City -- but there was a problem. Taylor, our baby, had become seriously ill, to the point that we were not sure he was going to make it. The doctors struggled trying to figure out what the problem was until they discovered he was very allergic to the protein in milk. We switched him to a special formula and moved on.

Oklahoma City was easier for me to adjust to. By now I knew the school drill for Jay, found the doctors we would need and a house to rent. I had started doing Mary Kay on the side on a part-time basis, meaning I wasn't doing much with it at all. This was the early 90s and the oil and gas industry was terrible, even though Dennis was in management. As soon as all the boys were in school, I started working outside of the home. I can't say there was a glass ceiling in the three companies I worked for, but it was certainly colored blue. I was working in sales, something I was pretty good at, and I enjoyed working with my customers. After disparaging incidents with pay cuts and dirty politics within the corporation, I decided I had had enough. I listened to their excuses, did the math, and decided if I was going to take a $16,000 per year pay cut, I could do better working for myself. I turned my computer in and went home.

I'm not one to sit around idly so I found myself working in the yard, pulling weeds, and carrying mulch. None of these were my favorites plus I had injured my back hauling heavy bags so I decided the weeds could take care of themselves. Mary Kay was looking good. I wanted to make my own money and have flexibility. I could have all of that if I applied myself once again.

The second time around with Mary Kay has been the best. I have been more diligent in the work, feeling confident that we are in Oklahoma City to stay. My personal sales in the last two years have earned me two beautiful rings and I have been in Mary Kay's Prestigious Queen's Court of Personal Sales during this time. I have my sights set on becoming a Mary Kay Sales Director and I would love to sport around town in a pink Cadillac. But there is more to it than that.

Mary Kay can change a woman's life, no matter the socioeconomic class she is in. My goal is to build a team of working women—those who will work Mary Kay and not just poke it with a stick—so they can enjoy the freedom of making their own spending money, the socialization of being with other women and realize their dream to own a business. Any woman—usually it is just women, but men can join too—can become a Mary Kay representative because the entry price is low and very affordable. There is nothing to lose and so much to gain. We have a 'Selling on the Go' program which gives flexibility, and there is a 100% money back guarantee for any customer that finds she doesn't like the product for any reason.

To grow my business, I knew I needed contact with people I wouldn't ordinarily meet. That meant I had to start doing some networking, but I didn't know for sure how that could happen. I heard about Gold Star Referral Clubs, and decided to see what the hub bub was all about. I love Gold Star! Not only has my business grown since I joined, but I met new friends, laughed a lot, and found new opportunities for my business.

I found my niche in corporate gifting of May Kay products. I make it easy for corporate leaders to bless their staff with a lovely gift basket of Mary Kay products and I have grown my business exponentially through using a private Facebook group. There are all kinds of ways to make Mary Kay work for you if you have the tenacity to stick with it. As for me, the mantra I've developed is, "Your age is your business. How you look is my business."

Brett Lorton

Owner

Home, Commercial Inspections

I've been asked how a boy from Greenfield, Illinois ended up in Oklahoma. Distance wise, it isn't that far but the journey did take some time. I think of it as climbing a ladder that at times is very well stabilized and other times… not so much. You keep climbing no matter what. Life isn't without risks.

My dad worked for farmers during my early years. At the end of 1st grade, we moved to Camp Warren Levis, a Boy Scout Camp in Godfrey, Illinois. Dad was hired as the camp ranger to basically take care of everything and anything. For me, I was too young to understand where I had landed. A 1,000-acre Boy Scout Camp with a hundred-acre lake that features all kinds of outdoor activities including swimming, hiking, archery—you know, the activities that help scouts earn their badges and start their journey to manhood. To say it was a great place to grow up would be an understatement. There was a lot of work attached to it that provided opportunities to learn. Including but not limited to cooking, fixing, mending, and repairing everything from simple equipment to the more complicated. My dad's philosophy was "The worst we can do is mess it up and need an expert, so let's try to fix it ourselves." He took it apart, figured out what was wrong with it and made it work. If he did throw something away, it was always in pieces when it was finally discarded because I had dissected every piece of it just to see how it was made.

My grandfather had the same philosophy as my father. If it breaks, fix it. I learned to build, plumb, wire, fix engines, you name it, I was exposed to it.

My older brother, Brad, and I graduated from Alton Senior High which had great vocational programs. Since I learned to weld at camp and my grandfather's farm and enjoyed it, I decided that I would take vocational welding from a great teacher. I used that skill to pay my tuition for engineering college. I also liked drafting and was lucky enough to have another great teacher, just like my welding instructor, who taught me the ins and outs of drafting.

So, I did the drafting and the welding classes. Along with all the other things I'd been learning from working with my dad and grandfather, not ever thinking it would lead to a career choice for me down the road.

Not long after I graduated from high school, my grandfather was killed in a car accident. My mother and I moved to the farm and took over running it for my grandmother. It was a working farm complete with crops, cattle, chickens, geese, and ducks. Everything but pigs. My grandfather didn't like them. Dad moved to the farm with us while the estate was settled.

My dad and I both got a job working for a nearby family business that serviced grain elevators. Once again, I was using my welding skills and enjoying the work. I was saving money for my future education. I loved working with my father for that year at the farm and the elevator company.

I enrolled in a two-year program at Ranken Technical Institute in the mechanical engineering department. It was a good school with an excellent placement rating and that's what I wanted, a path to a career. I had a job before I graduated.

I worked at A. O. Smith between school years as a welder. This company made frames for GM cars and trucks. I worked for them knowing there were opportunities beyond production. I moved into management as a Quality Control Supervisor in the press area. Automotive companies were testing adhesive and spot welding (unibody) to reduce cost and improve safety. This led to a shutdown of the plant.

> The more you care, the stronger you can be.

From there, I kind of bounced around. I was an Aldi Food Store manager. I did welding, some engineering and ended up at MacDonnell Douglas in St. Louis to work in the fighter plane program as a tooling engineer. I worked on various fighter aircraft programs (F15E, C17, F18, ATF, A12 and the Harrier). Defense programs were slowing down, so I transferred to a division of McDonnell Douglas that provided drafting/manufacturing software to engineering/manufacturing companies. I started as a trainer/consultant and then managed a consulting group that was deployed to manufacturing companies to train their engineers.

There was a company in Salt Lake City that was looking for an operations manager. I joined them as an Operations Manager and we opened an engineering facility in Brasov, Romania where engineers created digital models and drawings for companies with legacy data issues.

I met my wife during my time at McDonnell Douglas and our son, Brian, was born in 1989. That was my proudest moment. Brian was diagnosed with Epilepsy at six months and struggled along with the doctors to keep him alive. Through many drugs and finally diet, his health started to improve at two years old. I had the career position as my wife stayed home to care for Brian. We moved to my wife's home state of Oklahoma in 2001 and changed roles. I started working part time in insurance and securities and my wife worked for a retail consulting company as a financial analyst.

My wife decided to leave Brian and me in 2004. My part-time business wasn't going to provide enough income to sustain us, so I had to make some decisions. A friend had an oil exploration company and one day he asked me, "Have you ever thought of being a landman?"

I didn't even know what a landman was, but he assured me that with my engineering background I would be good at it. He reminded me that since I was good at using Excel, I would be good at doing this type of research work. At that time, it worked out well since Brian was staying with his mom during the week and riding the bus to school. I would pick Brian up and have him for the weekends. This allowed me to work full-time as a landman, which I did for several different brokerages. Once Brian graduated high school, he moved in with me full time.

In the meantime, another friend of mine owned a home inspection business. He had been doing it eight years and really liked it. We had been working together on building a smoker in his back yard when he began telling me about the home inspection business.

After the many slowdowns in oil and gas over the years, I decided to make a change. With what my grandfather and father had taught me about construction including roofing, framing, plumbing, wiring, pouring concrete, and let's not forget digging ditches, along with common sense made home inspection a natural fit. After a year of tutoring from my friend, studying while running title, I was ready. My mother wintered with us at that time and was the only reason I was able to pull the transition. The world lost a great lady, my mother, and an amazing human when she passed. Love you, Mom. I got my inspection license, and I opened On Target Home Inspections, LLC.

One of the best referral stories I have is about a house southeast of Purcell that I inspected three times. It started with the original family who was given my name by their realtor. After their stay, they gave my name and number to the proposed buyers. They had lived there a year and gave my name to the next buyer who called me to provide their home inspection. All three were a result of life changes.

I really don't know how to answer people when they ask when I plan on retiring. I feel like I already have. The saying is true, "If you find something you love, you'll never work another day in your life." Truer words have never been spoken. Love God, love my life, love my son, love my family, love my friends who have helped and supported me through thick and thin. I can't begin to thank my realtors and clients enough. Also, I can't wait to see what the future holds.

I know Gold Star Referral Club will remain in my life as a source, not only of business growth, but as some of the best friends I have ever had. Gold Star has helped me grow my business through referrals and I have had the privilege of helping others do the same. It is good to know people whom you can confidently refer to your clients.

David Nixon

Owner - Licensed Life & Health Agent

Nixon Insurance Agency

DavidNixonInsurance.com

1905 Windsong Drive
Oklahoma City, OK 73130

405-205-1149

dnixon4@att.net

"I'm not moving to Florida! Alligators will eat my grandchildren!"

A friend of mine thought about retiring to Florida but refuses on the grounds alligators will probably eat her grandchildren. I realize she's being overly dramatic, but she can picture alligators sneaking out of ponds, grabbing her granddaughter by the leg, pulling her into the pond, and having a healthy snack.

When she told me this, I laughed out loud. On average, there is one death per year in Florida due to alligator attacks.

The truth is, most alligator attacks are provoked and most of the time, it's males between the ages of sixteen and twenty-four doing the provoking. Why? Because the frontal lobe of a male's brain isn't fully developed and most often, they act without comprehending the consequences. This information alone is the best argument for covering the young men in your life with accident insurance.

Did you watch the scenes in Happy Gilmore about the alligator? Both Happy and Chubbs take on the alligator. Both are male. Both said, "Damn the consequences, let's have some fun!" And both went after the same alligator.

Shoot, as kids, my brother and I would jump off the roof for fun. What were we thinking? We weren't.

Therefore, young men need insurance. Seriously, though, I have sons. Enough said.

My parents are getting older, and my mom has an outright inability to say no to anyone—ever. I won't tell you their names or their address because, well, she'd probably purchase a used canoe full of holes from you if she thought it would help you. I'm not saying you have a holey canoe to sell, nor am I saying you'd try to sell her one, but who knows who might pick this book up, right? I'm just stating facts.

I cannot tell you how many times I have had to undo a purchase she's made. I love her. She has a heart of gold, and she loves people. However, the story does not end there. Because of her heart, she tends to get taken advantage of. I think we all know someone like my mother.

My father would come home to boxes of girl scout cookies, bags of popcorn, candles, chocolates, cookie dough, hot dogs, and anything else a child with an expectant gleam in their eyes would come a knockin' sellin'. She could not say no. My brother and I didn't care. We ate well.

Now that I'm older, I do care. A son grows up, becomes a man, and starts seeing the world through a man's eyes. Besides, the stakes have gone up quite a bit. It was no longer children knocking expecting a cookie sale. It was grown adults preying on the vulnerable, and I wasn't having it. I had to protect my mother.

I knew if my own mother was being taken advantage of, there were millions more who were also being taken advantage of. I had to do something. I could not sit idly by. The question became, how could I help?

Every industry has their bad seeds. You know what I mean. The man or woman who gives that industry a bad rap through their misrepresentation. Car salesmen and insurance salesmen are at the top of that list. I'm not saying every car salesman, or every insurance salesman are bad seeds out to take advantage of people. But I do know there are a lot of shady people out there.

Insurance salesman after insurance salesman sold my mother a policy she didn't need. I would have to unravel the red tape and find ways to cancel the policies and get her money returned. Don't get me wrong, my mother is a smart woman. Under normal circumstances, buying multiple policies or even changing policies wouldn't be an issue, but my mother has dementia. She forgets things and is confused. A salesman would have an easy time convincing her she wasn't protected. And the last thing she would want to do is burden my brother and me.

Finally, I decided if I couldn't beat them, then why not fight fire with fire? I studied for and passed my insurance examination.

First, let me say I already had a good career. I joined the military and served more than twenty-five years in the Army Band—both the Army Reserve Band and the

Army Band. I was a band director for sixteen years. After I hurt my back and could no longer stand for the long hours needed from a band director, I returned to my military background and started contracting. Contracting is a hit or miss kind of thing.

You can work consistently for a year, two years, then be off for a month, or even a year. The money is good when you're working, much better than teaching but it can be inconsistent.

Even with the inconsistencies in pay, I didn't start selling insurance to make money. I started selling insurance to help protect the vulnerable and to save people money.

Finally, I was in a position where I could help people—especially seniors—navigate their life insurance needs without signing their houses away.

Some corporations have a toxic atmosphere. The slimy salesmen I mentioned above are often encouraged to use nefarious methods to make a sale. That is the culture a company develops when their top priority is profit over people.

Other companies truly have the customer's needs at the top of their list of priorities. They will bend over backwards to help a client and will sacrifice the sale if they know the product isn't right for the client.

Over time, this company will be the most successful. Maybe not monetarily, but in customer satisfaction.

For me, insurance has never been about making money, so I didn't have to worry about toxic principles rubbing off on me.

The first company I worked for wasn't a good fit. I was a captive agent and sometimes finding the right policies for my clients was next to impossible. The company tended to fit in the money first category which went against everything I stood for. I needed the freedom to shop around for my clients, so I could find the best products for them.

It was about then I ran into a friend of mine, and he told me about another insurance company that put the needs of their clients first. I was intrigued. This was what I had been looking for.

Now, I get to help people save money, sometimes enough money to make a car payment, or even a house payment.

I recently worked with a couple who were paying almost $2000 a month for a Medicare supplemental policy. Neither one of them was sick nor had any history of chronic diseases. I showed them an MA plan and their premium went from nearly $2000 a month to $25 a month. They were ecstatic. Basically, I saved them a house payment. And they could afford to go on a vacation, which they hadn't been able to do in a long, long time.

Several months after I got my life and health insurance license, I joined Gold Star Referral Clubs. My goal was to replace the income I was getting from being in the Army Reserves. I've basically done that. I haven't knocked on doors or cold called anyone. All my business has come from referrals. All these referrals have given me the opportunity to meet people and hear their stories. People love to talk. They love to share about their lives and there are a lot of lonely people out there. I go in to help people save money and to make sure their health care needs will be taken care of should they ever need it. On occasion, I go to a person's home, and they have exactly what they need. There's just no reason to change anything so I don't. But when I leave, I always leave as a friend.

> # Leave the world better than we found it!

I see so many companies that do right by their employees but charge a premium to protect their families. How does this help their employees? My policies are so much easier on the family.

My very first customer was from Gold Star. He's a massage therapist and is still with me. I saved him about $500 a month. That's a car payment or a nice vacation at the end of the year. Any time I can save anyone any money, I feel good. And I sleep very well at night. That's a good place to be in.

If you would like to see how I might help you save some money, I'd love to sit down with you and look at your health care policy. Who knows, I might be able to save you a car payment.

Dawna Terrell

Independent Consultant and District Manager

Arbonne

dawnaterrell.arbonne.com

I work out of my home in:
Edmond, OK 73013

405-830-7362

terrelldawna@gmail.com

I never thought I would be an entrepreneur. I knew I wanted a college education, a family, and a stable life that allowed me and my family to do the things we wanted to do and be comfortable which pretty much mirrored that of my parents and grandparents lives. Like them, I grew up on a small farm southwest of Oklahoma City on State Highway 37, in the small farm community of Minco. Both of my parents grew up there, on country farms but on opposite sides of town. When I was three and my brother was six, they bought a small farm near both sets of grandparents and that's where I was raised.

My parents were high school sweethearts and have been married for over fifty-five years. Dad retired from Tinker Air Force Base in Midwest City after thirty-five years. My mother was home with us until I was in 7th grade. Then, an opportunity to go back to work at Tinker AFB opened and she took it, retiring from there in 2003, just a couple of weeks before my daughter, Rebecca, was born.

I loved the farm. I loved helping with the chores, the gardens and all that farm life entailed. I even enjoyed scooping poop from the cows on my grandparents' dairy farm. I loved the annual sweet corn harvest time with close and distant family, which occured around the 4th of July. So much of our food was home grown in the garden with fresh milk and beef from the dairy farm. We ate fresh produce, canned what we didn't need, storing it away in my grandparent's root cellar. When I finished high school, I moved to El Reno, sixteen miles away, to start college at Redlands Community College. I had to learn how to buy milk, beef, most vegetables, and some fruit in the grocery store. It was a shock.

Like most college kids, I needed a job which I found working at Hardee's fast-food restaurant in El Reno. That's where I met my husband, Mathew. He was three years older than me and had grown up in El Reno. We hit it off right away and started dating. When I finished at Redlands and moved to Edmond to start my next two years at University of Central Oklahoma (UCO), he did the same.

> # Helping you take the next step in your health and well-being!

We married in 1997 and I started my twenty-five-year higher education career at UCO. I completed my bachelor's degree a year later and my master's degree in 2000. We had our first child, Rebecca, in 2003 which is the same year Mathew started working at Tinker Air Force Base. All around, it was a good year for all of us. Five years later in 2008, we added our son, Benjamin, to our family. Mathew continued his career at Tinker Air Force Base in the Point of Use division and finished his bachelor's degree in industrial safety in 2013.

I grew up in church and my faith is very important to me. I love serving people. My family is the same, we all have servant hearts. In the summer of 2015, when my daughter was twelve years old and part of the youth group at church, they were planning a mission trip to Haiti. Both she and I prayed about going and we both felt lead to go and serve. While there, we would get to help the local ministers with Vacation Bible School (VBS) in Leveque to teach the Haitian children about God, to love on them, play with them, and to feed them. We would also plant some fruit bearing trees and water filtering systems for buckets.

But, before we could go, Rebecca had to raise the money to pay her own way. Under a banner of "Cinnamon Rolls for Haiti", we started selling cinnamon rolls to the congregants of our church as well as family and friends and those in the community. With the help of her very dear friends—and their moms—we rolled up our sleeves and made eighty-five dozen cinnamon rolls—over 1,000—all on one very long Saturday, gratefully using the church's commercial kitchen. Then, we delivered them on Sunday. It was a lot of hard work and an exhausting weekend but extremely worth it for the memories made with our friends and teaching Rebecca the value of working hard and appreciating those who helped us and those who supported her by buying a dozen, or two, or three. In fact, Cinnamon Rolls for Haiti not only paid her way but mine as well.

The trip to Haiti was a life-changing event for both of us and we knew in our hearts we were going back the next year with the church; however, that trip fell through. The VBS program the year before had been a great success. The children came in large numbers, especially as the week progressed and their parents learned they would be fed, which for most would be their only meal for the day. Many of them were still living in blue tarp tent homes years after the 2010 7.0 earthquake and it was heartbreaking. Rebecca and I talked to our minister about options for us to go even though the planned trip had canceled. Haiti is a dangerous country, especially for women to be traveling alone. He offered to go with us or we could go by ourselves, or with our friend Betsy who was planning a trip. I wasn't sure what to do but we agreed to pray about it. I knew in my heart we were going, one way or the other.

Our friend Betsy also has a heart for missions, and she shared with us about her plans to go to Haiti with a group from Arbonne and we were welcome to join them. All they asked is that we take part in a fundraiser to help build ninety homes for the Haitians who were still living in blue tarp tent homes. I didn't know that much about Arbonne but I deeply cared about the

Haitians, and so did Rebecca. Over the years I had only bought three Arbonne products from Betsy and that was the limit of my knowledge about Arbonne. After learning more about Betsy's trip, I gave Rebecca the choice. Whatever decision she made would determine how we would go. She chose for us to go with Betsy and the Arbonne group. I certainly didn't know anything about the company, but I knew Betsy.

It was another life-changing experience and most definitely the right decision. The people we traveled with were amazing. It was a similar, yet different, experience than the previous year. We had the opportunity to serve in a different Haitian community, Minotrie, meeting more families, serving food, and helping to paint some of the homes we funded. Part of the purpose for the fundraising was also to provide Haitians with jobs so we didn't want to take away that work. It was amazing to see and be in the community of homes that were built as part of our fundraising efforts. We also got to meet some of the families that were going to be given the protection of a safe home.

The Arbonne people were kind, loving, and committed to helping and ministering to the people of Haiti. They went with the same purity of heart that missions-oriented people have.

During this trip, I became dehydrated. I do not want to go into a lot of detail, but I can say that the heat was brutal and I did not drink enough water. I didn't know the symptoms for dehydration but I learned them – quickly – and I also had a lot of personal and up-close experiences with concrete out houses! Let me say, concrete outhouses in the heat of the summer are a torturous experience. All in all, it gave me even more compassion for the Haitians, and a better understanding of their lifestyle.

Since we were with a group from Arbonne you would think there would be conversations about Arbonne, the products and/or the business. But there wasn't. After we had spent the day out amongst the people, we would get together for a debriefing of the day's experiences each night, then everyone did their own thing. Those in Arbonne would have team meetings and Rebecca and I would go back to our cabin to shower, relax, and think about our day. I appreciated that so much.

When we returned to the states, Mathew drove to Dallas to pick us up – we had flown in and out of there to save money. On the drive back to Oklahoma City I began to think about starting my own Arbonne business and felt an overwhelming conviction that I was supposed to do this to be able to do more missions and serve others. It was a very strong and memorable moment I will never forget. So, now I was embracing Arbonne. This scared me. I had never considered owning my own business and I didn't think I wanted to, but the conviction was so strong that I knew God had a plan. I told Mathew and he was very supportive. I thought he would surely question the idea, but he didn't.

The next day I called Betsy. I told her I was starting my own Arbonne business. She was pleasantly surprised. She had never talked to me about other Arbonne products let alone the business opportunity. I shared about my conviction, my thoughts, my hesitations, my encouragements, and MY WHY.

Next, I told my parents who were both supportive and my mom even said, "I always thought you would be great at owning your own business." Ha! In fact, not one person tried to talk me out of it. Every single person that would be brutally honest with me, and I would value their input, was very encouraging, so it was confirmed…I was REALLY GOING TO DO THIS!

I am so thankful for the experience in Haiti and to learn how Arbonne made the trip possible through connections, community, and their business income. In addition, I got to see first-hand that their focus was to serve and help others out of pure love. My heart for Haiti combined with experiencing how others used Arbonne as their vehicle to help and serve others is why I experienced a conviction so strong that I absolutely could not say no.

So, I started my Arbonne business July 1, 2016, just five days after returning from Haiti and I have not once regretted my decision. God has blessed me through my business with not only the additional income but more importantly my health has improved, my community has grown, my personal and professional growth has flourished, and my opportunities to help and serve others has expanded. Doing more missions and serving others is my first why but since I started my business, my why continues to grow and I am so excited to see how it will change my life and those around me that I get to help and serve.

My twenty-five year career at UCO ended October 28, 2022, but a new and exciting career at Factor 110, the region's leader in event and destination management, began on November 7, 2022, alongside my Arbonne business.

I am excited to continue growing my Arbonne business and thoroughly enjoy and benefit from being a member of the Goldstar Uptown Club and the opportunity it has given me to push me outside my comfort zone, develop and practice a 60 second speech, improve my networking skills, expand my connections, and cultivate relationships with like-minded business owners who have a desire to give, then receive, and support each other. I love being able to refer contact information of the people I know and can trust to meet the various needs of my friends, family, and anyone I meet along the way.

Danielle Hill

Owner

Shelter Insurance Agency

shelterinsurance.com/CA/agent/DANIELLEHILL

1704 South Boulard Ste A
Edmond, Ok 73013

405-340-5606

daniellehill@shelterinsurance.com

"We're moving?" I could not believe it. I had lived most of my life in Shawnee, Oklahoma and now my parents are telling me we are moving to the city! This was where my friends were, my church, my life was here in this small town where our family was well known. "Why are we moving?" I am sure my ten-year-old mind was not comprehending what my parents were telling me or why.

My parents did everything they could to make the transition from Shawnee to Edmond easy for us. We had been living in a large, nice home but now we were sizing down, and dad was starting a new business. I was too young at the time to understand the stress and magnitude of this decision on a young family, but I knew that the change was hard on all of us.

> # Do the right thing,
> # no matter what.

That fall, my parents were totally committed to making this transition as easy for us as they could. It was hard to be the "new kid" in town in every situation, from sports, to school, to church. But we were a close-knit family, and I was able to see so many good things happen from these hard changes.

Dad had taken a job as an agency owner working for Shelter Insurance, in Edmond, and it was several years before we were on a solid financial foundation again. For the first few months, until our house sold in Shawnee, each morning Dad would drive us to our new schools in Edmond then that evening we would drive back to Shawnee, about an hour each way provided traffic and the weather cooperated. This continued until we could finally officially move. I don't think any of the three—my sisters and I—appreciated the sacrifice they were making nor the struggle they were enduring to make the change easier for us. That's what parents do.

Eventually, things got easier. We moved several times, each time to a little bigger and nicer home. I don't think it even occurred to me that we were renting a house until much later, when I was older. Looking back now, I realize my parents made a tremendous sacrifice for us and were starting over at an age when most adults begin to feel a little financial security in their lives.

Of the three sisters, I am the most like my dad in personality. My two sisters are both successful in their own endeavors and were not ever interested in the insurance business. I always knew I wanted a career. When I was in high school, I would work in my dad's insurance office, filing and doing the things that 'women did' in those days. Most of the women in the industry back then were producers for agency owners or worked alongside their husbands, and it was rare to see a woman own an agency.

After college, I continued working in my dad's insurance office, but this time I was a licensed producer selling insurance and I loved it. When I got pregnant with our first child, I took some time off from the insurance office. Then, when my husband's job required us to move to Tulsa, I worked for an independent agent doing Oil and Gas Insurance. I loved learning how other insurance agencies and carriers worked, but God had a different plan for me.

We moved back to Oklahoma City, and I felt called into fulltime ministry and eventually working with children in the inner-city ministries in downtown Oklahoma City as a children's director/coordinator. I found the work fulfilling and the opportunity for ministering was endless, which I loved and did for fourteen years.

In 2016, my dad approached me and asked me to come back to the insurance agency so he could begin to position himself for retirement. This had truly not been on my radar, since it had been a few years since I had worked in the industry. However, in my years of experience in ministry, I had learned how to manage people and events effectively for a common purpose and he felt that would translate well into agency ownership.

I struggled with this decision, and I prayed long and hard about it. Finally, I concluded that I should honor my mother and father and the work they had established and that, in and of itself, was ministry to my parents and my family. I accepted the offer and hit the ground running. As it turned out, I love the insurance business. I love helping people and this is a wonderful way to do it. Perhaps one day one of my three sons will follow in the footsteps of my dad and me by coming into the insurance business with me. Right now, that is far from their minds. Our oldest son, Cooper, is a singer/songwriter living in Nashville, Eli is a Senior and plays football and baseball and wants to be a pilot, and our youngest son, Lincoln, is an avid fisherman and basketball player. All three of them bring my husband of 20+ years, Jonathan, and myself immense joy and pride.

Gold Star Referral Clubs have been a great blessing to myself and my business. I have met so many wonderful people through the club and they have all become friends as well as business cheerleaders. We get to know each other, learn what it is each of us does in our field of expertise and then refer our clients who have those needs to our Gold Star members. It is always wonderful to get positive feedback from those clients.

One of my favorite referrals, not necessarily from Gold Star, but from an organization I am working with through several churches, is in helping immigrants or refugees from Afghanistan who have come here and settled in the inner-city area. They do not understand our laws and feel a great deal of confusion over them.

They did not have insurance in their native country, so they come to us not understanding the reason for the requirement here or anything about insurance. There is always a language barrier, so we have learned to get Catholic Charities on the phone to help us translate to our new clients, explaining the laws to them and helping them find their way through the insurance maze. What normally would take me about fifteen minutes to write an auto insurance policy takes at least an hour with them, but it is a wonderfully fulfilling feeling to see them walk out of our office with a smile on their face, knowing they are satisfied in what they've learned in that hour and that they'll be back and, most likely, bring a friend with them. That is a good feeling, and it is a form of ministry. God is good and so is the business he has placed me in.

When I was about ten years old, my dad sent me a postcard which I have kept in my office drawer. He was attending agency school in Columbia, Missouri for Shelter, and he told me he was sad to miss my softball game, but he felt the new job would be worth it in the end for our entire family. The year was 1988. It's 2023, and I have earned my contract with Shelter and qualified as the top 10% of the company in the last two years. I think it was worth it dad, don't you?

Nathan Acker

Owner

ACE Handyman Services

acehandymanservices.com/offices/edmond-and-north-oklahoma-city

100 NW 150th St Suite C-2
Edmond, OK 73013

405-861-8300

nacke@acehandymanservices.com

I was born and raised in eastern New Mexico in the little town of Portales, which hugs the Texas border. Although we are small, with a 2010 population of 12,280, we boast a great university – Eastern New Mexico University – and we are only thirteen miles from Cannon Air Force Base. It is a great little town that offers much considering its size.

My parents were hard workers. Dad owned a Daylight Donut shop for thirty-two years as well as several rental properties. I worked at the donut shop every weekend from the time I was thirteen until I graduated from high school. I learned about business by working at the donut shop and helping him take care of the rental properties which I believe helps me a great deal now. I don't know how to do everything but I do have a pretty good understanding of how things work. My mom worked at the university – it is a Division Two size university – and she was the accounts director for several years.

Our little town had a special program where if you graduated from high school with a 3.0 or higher-grade point, they would pay for your college education. That worked well for me. I was able to stay at home, go to school and graduate with no debt, which really helped me be financially prepared for life. What I had not counted on was getting sick. I was in college, and everything was going well until I suddenly got sick – really sick. As it turned out, I was twenty-one years old and diagnosed with Type I diabetes, juvenile diabetes. That was a little unusual but once they figured it out, I was put on insulin and was able to move on with my life. Both of my parents are quite slim, as am I, so it was a huge surprise when we found out I was diabetic.

Although I don't look like it, being so tall and thin, I've always been sports oriented. I played basketball and tennis from the time I was ten years old. Now I encourage my sons to do the same. They are a little slow on the upstart, but they are getting there.

I married my wife – Terrah – while I was in college. She is amazing and a great asset for me. We had our first child, Ethan, right away. That was a great thing for me because I needed to be grounded. I had been sick and was in my fifth year of college when he came along. I realized he was my responsibility and I needed to get anchored and on with a career to provide for my family.

Geology is a field that always interested me, so I graduated with an environmental science and geology degree with a minor in business. My younger brother went to OSU at Stillwater to finish his degree and I decided that was a good idea so I followed suit. I graduated in December 2012 and two weeks later I had a job working in the oil fields for Chesapeake Energy Company. It didn't matter that I had a geology degree, it was required that I prove myself to the company, so they put me on an oil derrick in the panhandle of

Oklahoma where we were pretty much isolated from everything. By now, Terrah was pregnant with our second child – McCray – and was spending a great deal of time alone in our mobile home waiting for the baby to be born. It wasn't fair to her, and I knew I needed to make some changes.

After a year in the oil fields, I was transferred into Chesapeake's office in Oklahoma City where I worked for five years, then I worked for a small operator for three years, doing technical work as an operations geologist. They wanted to put me on a contract so I agreed; I still do that from time-to-time. But always, in the back of my mind was the desire to be a business owner like my dad. The oil industry is up and down, and it isn't unheard of to get laid off which happened to me - twice. After the second lay off, which was on our 10th anniversary, it was time to decide to find something else to do.

My college experience prepared me for owning a business, in terms of time management, knowing the details and being organized. I had not only worked for my dad, but I had worked at ACE Hardware as well. When the second layoff happened in the oil industry; I knew it was time to do something different.

ACE had bought out a business called Handyman Services and were offering franchises. I knew almost immediately I wanted to do it, but it took me three months before I was willing to sign the papers and take the next step. That was in 2021. Now we employ five craftsmen plus myself and my wife who works part time in the office.

We love Oklahoma. The people here are amazing, friendly, and inclusive. There is a lot to do and we enjoy doing it with our boys. We do travel some. I recently took my family to Chicago on a business trip. It was odd. I didn't feel threatened but I didn't feel safe and I was glad to get home. When I was in the oil industry, we could have moved to Houston or Midland, Texas, but we chose to stay here because it is a great place to raise a family.

> # If opportunity doesn't knock, build a door!

Our office is small, but that isn't the point. The work we do, the skills and abilities of our craftsmen is what's important. We send them out to do a job – mostly in the Edmond and North Oklahoma City area -- and we need to know they are not only going to do it well but they have a servant's heart. That is what I look for when I'm hiring people – do they care about others and are they willing to go the extra step to help people.

Most of our craftsmen come with their own tools, trucks, and know-how. I do interview them at length to see if they fit our business profile. We've had a few missteps with employees but they don't last long. We are very focused on doing a job and doing it right the first time. Customer service is everything to me and I always want our clients to let me know if there is a problem.

My best craftsmen are the ones who were auto mechanics in the beginning of their careers. They learned how to fix things, how to put things back together and to make sure it runs well. After that, they stepped into being craftsmen whether it was intentional or accidental, but they make great employees. We appreciate that.

If I find a job is going too slow, for whatever reason, I'll go to the job site, pick up a hammer and start helping. That always seems to speed it up. Our customers are paying by the hour and I'm very cognizant of that. Good work done in a good and fair time frame is what I'm looking for in our craftsmen. I learned early on in this business that it is incumbent on me to check with our clients, to find out if they are happy with the work and there are no problems. Word of mouth is our best advertisement and we want to keep it positive.

Gold Star is a great referral organization. I heard about it when I was still considering buying my franchise. I called Jeff and inquired about it, went to a meeting and I've been here ever since. It is a great place to be when you are starting a business. Occasionally we run into something that is not in our purview as craftsmen, but through the auspices of Gold Star I always know there is someone that is skilled in that specific area, and we are happy to refer business to them. I find it always makes an impact on our customers as well when we tell them, "We don't do that particular work, but we know someone whom we can recommend that is highly qualified." The customer is happy to hear that and relaxes in our recommendation.

My family is my why. I started my business to have more time with them. Gold Star has helped me grow my business, allowing me to have more time together with my family.

Caleb Jackson

Owner

TradePros Oklahoma City and Tulsa

tradeprosokc.com

2408 SE 10th Place
Moore, OK 73160

405-249-7290

cjackson@tradeprosokc.com

We had a plan to become a successful HVAC company. But that was all it was. A plan. Then we got our first job, and were excited to be on our way. We bought an old used trailer, a white one that was a little banged up and had a sign on the side that said, "Pro Tech Pest Solutions", and a Dodge pickup truck with a beat-up front end, but we didn't care. We were pumped. We hadn't gone far on that first job until the trailer slipped off the hitch and slid about fifty feet before we came to a stop. That was our beginning. The craziness didn't bother us. The future was before us. We made $2,400 on that job which we split and put into the bank.

FEAR

F alse

E vidence

A ppearing

R eal

We worked like that through the first year. Get a job, go do it, split the money and be ready to reinvest it into the business. Toward the end of June 2019, it was time to commit to building the company. We had worked at it on the side for as long as we could, so we rented a 40 x 17 storage unit in Moore and that became our office and warehouse. We were there almost a year, even in thirty-degree weather. Kerry is amazing. He made a makeshift heater for us out of junk material we had removed from a job, and it managed to keep us warm enough to stay there through that winter and into the summer.

We had a little white table we got at Walmart that held our computer, printer, and office supplies. We had a set of shelves for our parts inventory. We didn't care. We knew we were building something, and we were okay with the inconvenience for the moment. Just before COVID hit, we moved across the street into a 1,000-foot office with a shop behind it. Now we had both places, and we were growing. We hired one guy and then two more and we were moving up.

That Memorial Day weekend we went camping, taking Curtis and Kris with us. They had their own heat and air business at the time, but we really wanted them to join us. The three of us—Kerry, Kris, and I—sat around the fire talking. Kerry and I had plans to bring Kris into the business with us if he would come but we weren't sure about what he would do since he had been in business with his dad. As it turned out, we ended up bringing both Kris and Curtis—brothers—into the business with us, and they are fantastic.

We had known each other for years. We went to high school together in Jones, Oklahoma, from my sophomore year on. We played football and they became my best friends. I knew they were great guys, totally trustworthy and that counted for a lot. We meshed well together. They are two guys without guile. They don't hold grudges; they know what they are doing in the HVAC business and all of this—their personalities and work ethics--makes them perfect business partners.

We continued to grow. In 2020 we had four people working for us then in 2021, at what seemed to be an overnight pace, we had twelve employees with ten people working here and two in Tulsa. We moved into a 6,000 square foot building where we are currently, but we are outgrowing this facility. Now we have twenty-one employees, and we are looking forward to more growth. Since the very beginning, everyone has worked at least forty hours a week year around and that is pretty phenomenal with all that has gone on with COVID, the economy and cutbacks everywhere else.

We want to be number one in the state. Our Tulsa office currently consists of 2,000 square feet of warehouse with two office spaces. We are seeing tremendous growth there as well. We are looking forward to the day when we will be the largest company of our kind in Oklahoma. We are expanding beyond HVAC. We are open to all types of trades including electrical, landscaping, windows and siding, roofing, and whatever fits into the Trade Pro specifications. We are a service-oriented company, and we intend to stay that way.

All of us are in our thirties. We have room and time to grow in the business and build it into something that Oklahoma will be proud of. We are a family-owned business with some of our wives and family members working behind the scenes in the office and elsewhere. They aren't here just because they are family; they are here because they know what they are doing, and they hold this business to an accountable level.

Kerry has been developing an idea in his head for years and now we have implemented it in our business. Basically, it is a subscription service for HVAC maintenance and repair. It is a simple, uncomplicated contract, where the customer agrees to pay $25 a month for the security of knowing we have their backs if something goes wrong with their HVAC unit. If the repair is $500 or less, it won't cost them anything more than the $25 a month they are currently paying. If is a more expensive repair, then they get a huge discount. It works well and people like it. Our society is used to paying for subscriptions to things like Netflix, HULU, and the like so why not a subscription for HVAC service that offers two maintenance services a year and the guarantee that we'll be there if they need us. We are not the most expensive company in the state, but we aren't the cheapest either. We price our services at a fair rate and supply good, clean, and rapid services for our customers. They are happy and we are happy.

I, personally, am not an HVAC person so my job is to market our business and I'm pretty good at it. I have experimented with all types of advertising, finding Google ads to be the most productive. That isn't the only place where we advertise though. We have used radio and TV as well as billboards. One of the things we have done is to come up with a recognizable jingle that plays when our ads pop up. This is primarily because people are not watching the ads, they are watching their devices, but the jingle is one that they relate to and, in turn, subconsciously connect it with us reminding them whom they should call if they have an HVAC problem. I think it is clever and it has helped in the growth department.

Another thing we have done is to become completely automated. How many times have you had a service person come to your home, do a repair, and give you a handwritten estimate or receipt that isn't legible? We don't do that. All our trucks are equipped with computerized devices that list the service and provide a professional printout that is totally legible, clean, and concise. People like that and we do as well.

We are not afraid to try new and different things. They don't always work but we do have the guts to try them. If something goes wrong, we analyze it, figure out what went wrong, learn from it, and move on. No one gets upset. We understand we are growing and there will be mistakes along the way. We have made the decision to take them into consideration and learn from them.

One of the best decisions we made a long time ago was to join Gold Star. I truly believe that is one of the reasons our business has grown so rapidly. We want to have a representative in every Gold Star in Oklahoma. If we expand into other states and there are Gold Star Referral Clubs there, we'll have someone joining them as well. Gold Star is good people, doing good things together and that is something that helps everyone.

Courtney Wilson

Owner / Solution Specialist

Big Dome Promotions

bigdomepromo.com

4425 E 31st St, Ste 210
Tulsa, OK 74135

405-408-2225

cwilson@bigdomepromo.com

"Courtney, we'd like you to help us launch a promo business."

That was not at all what I expected to hear on that January afternoon in 2021. Working for two entrepreneurial business partners, I was accustomed to new ideas of value-added offerings for our customers. This one came as a surprise, though. 2020 had been hard for the entire world, and the idea of launching a business amid overwhelming downturn and turmoil was both terrifying and exhilarating. Because positivity and finding fun in difficult places are core values for me, the exhilarating side prevailed, and a partnership was born!

The next few months were focused on learning the software and creating procedures and best practices for our team. We set up a launch team to collaborate on building the website and setting up our social platforms. We had a seasoned consultant of 30+ years in the promo industry helping us through the process of learning the industry and helping us avoid some rookie mistakes. Not that we didn't make any, of course, but each one had value in shaping our future actions.

We were finally ready for the big rollout to our sales team. Because of the other businesses within our organization, we have reps in many states throughout the country. Promotional products permeate throughout all industries, so Big Dome Promo brings us all together in our efforts to add value for our customers.

We've seen some great successes for our reps, including becoming a uniform provider for a baseball league, a T-shirt supplier for a cleaning franchise, and a branded apparel supplier for several businesses and resale shops. We've also partnered with a large company in providing swag for their all-employee conference, as well as countless opportunities to stock companies with trade show supplies, giveaways and everyday items branded with their logo.

> Faith, hope and love are the only things that last... a worthy investment to pursue in all areas of life.

We recently relaunched our website on a new platform that allows us to provide Showcase pages, which opens many exciting opportunities. One of my favorites is a company who preselected holiday gifts for their employees to choose from, as well as setting up an anniversary gift program. Several uniform programs are set up and school spirit stores are on the way!

Being a part of Gold Star Uptown Referral Club has been a great blessing to me. Not only are the members fun, but they are the best team ever for referring each other and helping us grow our business as we help them grow theirs. I recommend Gold Star Referral Clubs to anyone in business, whether they are just starting out or are well established.

I love what I do with Big Dome Promo, and I'm grateful for the opportunity. I love people, and I love helping them. I get to do this in all aspects, from internal operations to aiding our sales team to working with my own customers. It's humbling to look back and see how each job I've had has prepared me for all the things I'm doing now. I know it's not by accident and give God all the glory. Throughout the good times and the bad, He is my sustaining source of confidence, peace, and joy.

When you find yourself in need of promoting your business, gifting customers or employees, setting up a uniform store, or anything in between, I'd be honored to partner with you in making it a reality!

Whatever your brand needs... Big Dome has you covered!

Michael McGinley

Sales and Project Management

Altru Roofing

altruroofing.com

1132 S Sooner Road
Midwest City, OK 73110

405-826-9266

michael@altruroofing.com

My parents adopted me before I was born. They really wanted to bring me home from the hospital when I was first born but Oklahoma has a law that puts the adoptive child into foster care for two weeks to give the birth mother time to come to grips with and solidify her decision. Mom and Dad were solid, working people; Dad worked at Tinker Air Force base as a mechanical engineer and Mom had a master's degree in early education. They spoiled me, to some degree, but not as badly as you might think. They were in their thirties when they got me, so they were old enough and responsible enough not to make a mess of me, however because I was the youngest grandchild, I was beyond blessed at birthdays and Christmases by the rest of the family.

I grew up in Oklahoma City, graduated from Del City High School and have lived my life, for the most part, in and around the Oklahoma City metroplex. We traveled quite a bit when I was growing up and we loved it. We went to Hawaii, Alaska, Disney World, and other places that were not only fun but left a great sense of adventure within me. I grew up knowing when I got married and had my own family, I wanted to be able to take trips and explore together as a family like I had done with my parents.

My wife, Ashley, and I have two children, a boy, and a girl. Jaide, 14, and Grehson, 11. My wife wanted several children, but I knew if we had more, we wouldn't be able to travel and do the fun things with the kids that we are able to do with just two. We take nice vacations, alternating between what is fun and entertaining for them and what is fun and entertaining for us. One year we'll do a large vacation taking the four of us and then later in the year, Ashley and I will take a few days off for just the two of us. The next year, we will flip flop that with Ashley and I taking more time for ourselves on a larger vacation and a smaller scale holiday for the kids. It works out well that way and everyone seems to enjoy it.

I work for Noah Brown of Altru Roofing and Construction in Warr Acres. I am what you might call a front man in that I find and meet clients, build relationships, and stay in touch with them all through the roofing process. We find this brings them comfort and peace of mind knowing that someone they relate to is there, watching out over the work that is being done and staying in communication with the homeowner. The name Altru is a spin on altruism which means putting the needs of others first no matter the personal cost. Noah is big on that. Each year he takes a percentage of the profits of the company and donates them to a worthwhile project. Last year it was to a non-profit for veterans.

I haven't always been in the roofing and construction business. I started off working in the oil field for a company out of Canada by the name of Cougar Tool.

They had a shop here in Oklahoma City as well as one in Houston. I worked on shocks, hydro, mechanical tool jars and motors. From there, I went to Baker Hughes. Most of the tools were Measurement While Drilling (MWD) tools. MWD tools gather data downhole and send the information back to the surface.

> The name Altru is a spin on altruism, which means putting the needs of others first, no matter the personal cost.

I liked working in the oil fields, but the work wasn't steady. The first time I got laid off, my wife and I were caught a little unaware. When I got called back to work, we made sure we were prepared for layoffs the next time, which, of course, did happen. Then, there was the third lay off. By then, I knew I needed to change no matter how well the oil field work paid. I began looking around and that was when I decided to give Noah at Altru Roofing a call. Noah and I had worked together at Baker Hughes in the past. I work strictly on commission, so it took a while for me to build up my clientele and begin making decent money again. I think it was almost a year. I stuck it out though because I liked the work, meeting people and helping them through the uncertainties of new roofs and/or repairs to their existing roofs or other construction projects within their home.

One of the things I like best about my current job is the freedom it has given me. I don't punch a clock so I'm able to do a lot of the running for our kids, to their doctor and dentist appointments and the like. Plus, it allows me time to be there for them when they have an extra-curricular activity. It works well for all of us. My wife schedules their appointments and I work my appointments around theirs. Family is everything to us and this job allots me time to be with them.

On May 3, 1999, there was a huge tornado – an F-5 – that tore through Oklahoma, especially Moore, OK. My parents lost their home in that tornado. You know, when a tornado of that size comes through, it rips up and destroys everything, leaving very little that is salvageable. We lost things that had belonged to my grandparents, but everyone was okay and that was all that mattered. A few years later, in 2013, my wife and I were faced with our own tornado.

While we traditionally think of tornadoes being a night raider, this one came during the day and that is why so many school children were killed, even some teachers. I was working nights, so I was at home, asleep. Ashley woke me up and said we had to go. I didn't think it would do that much damage but the four of us got into our car – I hated that car – and drove to where we would be out of the projected path of the tornado. I left my truck at the house thinking nothing was going to happen. I was wrong. Everything was destroyed, including my truck; but we still had the hated car! Most importantly, we were fine. The four of us had survived. The only thing we lost was stuff and when it comes down to it, that isn't important.

We were blessed though. The company Ashley was working for at the time had a corporate apartment which they loaned to us. We stayed there two months, rent-free. That helped us a lot.

When I first started with Gold Star, I didn't know anything about networking. I heard about it as a referral program, and I thought it might be a help to me, so I decided to check it out. At first, it was all about me. What could I get out of it? I began listening to the ten-minute talks and I soon learned it wasn't all about me but about helping others achieve their goals and expanding their businesses. Pretty soon, I was meeting people on a one-on-one basis, learning about them and what they do, then recommending them to others.

One of the ladies, Sandy, works with Mary Kay. I'm a roofer! I didn't know how on earth I could help anyone that was doing Mary Kay but, as it turned out, some of my roofing clients were Mary Kay customers that had lost their representative, so I was able to give them Sandy's contact information. In turn, I've received a lot of referrals from Sandy for clients that needed home repair or roofing work done. It has worked very well.

One day I learned that Mary Kay does a special program for administrators of companies. I talked to Sandy, learned what they look for in a company and realized that my wife, a HR manager, was the very type of person she was looking for. I connected them, they met for lunch, became friends and now my wife also sells Mary Kay.

I have learned from my work in the roofing and construction business, and from Gold Star, that networking is essential to building a business. If people like you, like the work you do and are happy with the results, they will recommend you to others. That is the best way to build a business, the best type of advertising anyone can get, and I love it. I love helping others and being helped by them. Gold Star is a great program.

In Memoriam

Darlene Shortridge

Owner/Co-Founder

40 Day Publishing

40DayPublishing.com

PO Box 950794
Oklahoma City, OK 73195

405-588-7948 (Dan)

success@40daypublishing.com

"I'm sorry, but we're going to have to let you go."

The year was 2008 and the economy was on a downward spiral. We lived in Wisconsin in a city with a population of 60,000 people and every single business revolved around General Motors—including my husband's.

GM announced they were going to one shift. I knew then we'd be without an income. Sure enough, the next business day Dan received the call.

I should back up a little. In 2006, I wrote my first full length novel. It took me four months to write nearly 100,000 words. The story poured out of me. All I did was write. Afterward, since I knew absolutely nothing about the publishing industry, I placed my spiral bound masterpiece on a bookshelf to collect dust. It was the least I could do.

I dreamed of hand cramps from signing too many books, of seeing my name on the New York Times Best Seller's List (in fact, for the longest time I had Siri call me that on my phone), of walking into any store whatsoever and seeing my book on the shelves and dressing up for a red carpet stroll when my book became a movie. I knew how to dream big, but I didn't know how to make it happen. I was still under the impression if you write the book, they will read it. They did not.

By the time 2008 hit, I pretty much had resigned myself to being a one book wonder — it wasn't exactly a hit since I hadn't found a publisher for the story. I had such high expectations, and nothing was going the way I wanted it to. The loss of Dan's job was just one more disappointment. I stopped thinking about publishing my work and concentrated on surviving. My state of mind alternated between depression, anger, bitterness, and feeling sorry for myself. In fact, I could pretty much experience them all at once if I tried hard enough. I know, I'm talented.

We ended up moving north for a job Dan was promised. The weekend we moved we were notified the company decided against opening the office. There we were hours from family with no job, no income, and very little hope.

> "You can have everything in life you want if you will just help enough other people get what they want." — Zig Ziglar

Let me say this, I have the best husband in the entire world. He worked his butt off doing whatever he could find. The man delivered newspapers and pizza. He sold internet service door to door. He traveled all week-long taking directory pictures for churches. You name it, he did it. And he never grumbled (at least when I was within ear shot) and he always maintained a great attitude. I could not say the same for myself.

Two years passed. One day as we were driving home from church, snow piled high on the sides of the road, he turned to me and asked, "Are we going to do anything with your book? Do we believe in it?"

My answer was a resounding yes! Of course, I believed in my book.

In earnest, I began the search for a publisher. It took me a bit of time, but I ended up with three publishing offers. Two from what are called hybrid publishers and one from a traditional publisher. After extensively researching, we chose one of the hybrid publishers. Dan has always been an avid student of intellectual property and was against signing the rights to my book away. With a hybrid publisher, we retained all rights. This would prove very wise later.

To say I was excited was an understatement. All our money problems were about to vanish. I listed out the things I would replace — all the things I had to sell after he lost his job — and I waited for the royalty checks to start pouring in. I look back now and I have to chuckle. How naïve I was.

My highest royalty check was 19 bucks — that was for a three month period. It would have been $25 but apparently, I had a book returned. It was enough to buy some fast food. Again, disappointment set it.

After a year and a quarter of my expectations not being met, I looked at my husband and told him, "I'm going to take the rights to my book back. I'd rather give this thing away and help people than have it sit with a publisher doing nothing." I believe this decision was the absolute turning point in my career. This was when everything stopped being about me, about what I could get, about what I could buy, about what recognition I would receive…and it became about helping other people. There is a quote by Zig Ziglar (one of the best salesmen in all of history) that reads, "You can have everything in life you want if you will just help enough other people get what they want."

The publisher had my book priced so high no one was buying it. I was an unknown author with a book priced higher than pretty much every best-selling author with a book out. Let's face it, no one was going to buy my paperback book for $21.00. I knew that. My bank account knew that. My publisher knew that. The problem was, they didn't care. They got their money up front. Why would they care if my book was successful?

I sent a certified letter telling them to pull my book from distribution. The following 90 days were nearly unbearable. In the meantime, we readied my manuscript for publishing. On day 91, we uploaded my manuscript to Amazon. I then scheduled a three-day giveaway of my e-book over Mother's Day weekend, 2012. That was the weekend we moved to Oklahoma. What a sight we were. Riding in a little Toyota Echo with a carrier on top and every half hour, there I was trying to get a signal so I could check the number of downloads of my book. The number of giveaways kept climbing. As of that Monday morning, I had given away over 30,000 copies of my first novel. Reviews started pouring in. Sales shot through the roof. Until Forever hit number one on Amazon. I couldn't believe what we had accomplished. Neither could the rest of the publishing world.

I began hearing from authors all over the world who wanted to know what I did to accomplish such a feat. For one full year I simply helped people. I told them what I did and gave them advice on doing the same for their books. At one point, an author who we helped hit number one on Amazon told me, "Darlene, you have to do something with this. This is an open door to provide for your family."

Dan and I knew the truth of what she said, and we already had an appointment set with a retired OU professor and his wife. He had four manuscripts he'd written, and he had no idea what to do with them. We walked away with an agreement to publish his work. Now, ten years later, we have helped publish hundreds of books for hundreds of authors from around the world. We have helped grandmas writing poetry to moms writing children's illustrated picture books to famous people writing business principle books. We were finally seeing success. However, one thing was missing. Our local community still had no idea we were here. I knew our business could grow even more if our community got behind us.

I had attended one networking event fairly regularly but, even though I'm pretty outgoing, nothing much came of it. From that one experience I decided networking didn't work. Not being one to quit, when another opportunity presented itself, I attended. What can I say? I'm a glutton for punishment. This one was a much larger event. This event led me to the real world of networking — not just a social club for gossiping and eating — but a real networking organization — one that held fast to the same values I held, one that believed in serving and giving of yourself and your talents then trusting the process would grow your own business. I visited twice before I joined and the group was so vibrant, so full of energy, and so intentional, I received referrals immediately.

At first, I wasn't sure how I could help the members grow their businesses. Then, I really assessed my talents and knew how I could help. I could teach them the power of story. I have since received thousands of dollars in referrals from my fellow club members.

The beautiful thing is, while we all want to grow our businesses, we all want to simply help others. I remember one referral I was given. A woman had put together her family history and wanted to publish it so other family members could have a copy. I called her the same day I received the referral. She wasn't interested in selling copies, this was just for family. I knew my services were not what she needed. She didn't need a professional looking book. Something simple would suffice. I was more concerned with her meeting her end goal than lining my pockets.

I walked her through the basics and sent her a free copy of our book, 40 Day Publishing, so she could learn to do a very basic job of formatting and cover design to upload to Amazon. When I explained the process then told her how much each copy would cost her, she was in tears. She even called me the following day to thank me once again for caring about her and her project. To me, this is what being a part of Gold Star Referral Clubs is all about. And hearing that smile behind those tears made all the time spent well worth it.

The Gold Star Difference

"We're fun, friendly, and do serious business."

Gold Star members are Go-Givers. Gold Star members embrace the Go-Giving culture from the best-selling book, The Go-Giver, by Bob Burg and John David Mann. This culture of reciprocity is why Go-Givers sell more and have more fun doing it.

You will experience a purposeful agenda that is geared toward giving and receiving referrals. Our visitors say, *"It's fun but you get a lot done."*

Our referral meetings are not overly long. Meetings only last a little over an hour, usually during breakfast or lunch.

You can Cross-Club. You can visit other Gold Star Referral Clubs as much as you want if your industry is not already represented in that other Club.

Gold Star doesn't fine you for being late, not giving a referral each week, or missing a meeting!

Gold Star Club leaders have easy guidelines to follow and only serve six months at a time.

You can start a Gold Star Referral Club anywhere in the United States. When you find 3-5 core members and a place to meet, we will help you get the club going.

Our absence policy is understanding. You can use a substitute if you must miss a meeting.

We educate, train, and teach pro-active networking skills. Networking Success Training is given via email free to every member who joins. Gold Star corporate, based in Tulsa, OK, sends weekly business tips.

Every week the **Club Business Coach teaches a networking success tip.** Everything is online and easy to manage in the Member's Room.

We love inviting visitors. Everyone kicks in to help build your club and to increase referrals.

Finally, **we're happy to be different!** Gold Star Referral Club members have **contagiously upbeat** and positive attitudes. We're having fun networking and passing business referrals.

Learn how your organization can benefit from having a customized Business-Referral book…

www.GoldStarPress.com